Wood Pellet Smoker And Grill Tips And Tricks

Proven Strategies On How To Get The Best Out Of Your Wood
Pellet For Real Pitmasters With Delicious Recipes And Techniques
To Smoke Meats, Fish, And Vegetables

LIAM JONES

Table of Contents

BREAKFAST RECIPES

1. *Juicy Cheeseburger*

Preparation Time: 10 minutes

Cooking Time: 10 minutes

Servings: 6

Ingredients:

- 2 lbs. ground beef
- 1 egg beaten
- 1 Cup dry bread crumbs
- 3 tablespoons evaporated milk
- 2 tablespoons Worcestershire sauce
- 1 tablespoon Grilla Grills All Purpose Rub
- 4 slices of cheddar cheese
- 4 buns

Directions:

1. Start by consolidating the hamburger, egg, dissipated milk, Worcestershire and focus on a bowl. Utilize your hands to blend well. Partition this blend into 4 equivalent parts. At that point take every one of the 4 pieces and partition them into equal parts. Take every one of these little parts and smooth them. The objective is to have 8 equivalent level patties that you will at that point join into 4 burgers.

2. When you have your patties smoothed, place your cheddar in the center and afterward place the other patty over this and firmly squeeze the sides to seal. You may even need to push the meat back towards the inside a piece to shape a marginally thicker patty. The patties ought to be marginally bigger than a standard burger bun as they will recoil a bit during cooking.

3. Preheat your Kong to 300 degrees.

4. Keep in mind during flame broiling that you fundamentally have two meager patties, one on each side, so the **Cooking Time** ought not to have a place. You will cook these for 5 to 8mins per side—closer to 5mins on the off chance that you favor an uncommon burger or more towards 8mins if you like a well-to-done burger.

5. At the point when you flip the burgers, take a toothpick and penetrate the focal point of the burger to permit steam to get away. This will shield you from having a hit to out or having a visitor who gets a jaw consume from liquid cheddar as they take their first nibble.

6. Toss these on a pleasant roll and top with fixings that supplement whatever your burgers are loaded down with.

Nutrition: Calories: 300 Carbs: 33g Fat: 12g Protein: 15g

2. No-Flip Burgers

Preparation Time: 30 minutes

Cooking Time: 30 minutes

Servings: 2

Ingredients:

- Ground Beef Patties
- Grilla Grills Beef Rub
- Choice of Cheese
- Choice of Toppings
- Pretzel Buns

Directions:

1. To start, you'll need to begin with freezing yet not solidified meat patties. This will help guarantee that you don't overcook your burgers. Liberally sprinkle on our Beef Rub or All to Purpose Rub and delicately knead into the two sides of the patty. As another option, you can likewise season with salt and pepper and some garlic salt.

2. Preheat your wood pellet to 250 degrees Fahrenheit and cook for about 45mins. Contingent upon the thickness of your burgers you will need to keep an eye on them after around 30 to 45mins, yet there's no compelling reason to flip. For a medium to uncommon burger, we recommend cooking to about 155 degrees.

3. After the initial 30 to 40mins, if you like liquefied cheddar on your burger feel free to mix it up. Close your barbecue back up and let them wrap up for another 10mins before evacuating. For an additional punch of flavor, finish your burger off with a sprinkle of Grilla Grill's Gold 'N Bold sauce. Appreciate.

Nutrition: Calories: 190 Carbs: 17g Fat: 9g Protein: 13g

3. *Juicy Smokey Burger*

Preparation Time: 30 minutes

Cooking Time: 30 minutes

Servings: 2

Ingredients:

- 1 pound Beef
- 1/3 pound per burger
- Cheddar cheese
- Grilla AP Rub
- Salt
- Freshly Ground Black Pepper
- Hamburger Bun
- BBQ Sauce

Directions:

1. Split every 1/3 pound of meat, which is 2.66 ounces per half.
2. Level out one half to roughly six inches plate. Put wrecked of American cheddar, leaving 1/2 inch clear.
3. Put another portion of the meat on top, and seal edges. Rehash for all burgers.
4. Sprinkle with Grilla AP rub, salt, and pepper flame broil seasonings.

5. Smoke at 250 for 50mins. No compelling reason to turn.

6. Apply Smokey Dokey BBQ sauce, ideally a mustard-based sauce like Grilla Gold and Bold, or Sticky Fingers Carolina Classic. Cook for an extra 10 minutes, or to favored doneness.

Nutrition: Calories: 264 Carbs: 57g Fat: 2g Protein: 4g

FISH AND SEAFOOD RECIPES

4. *Teriyaki Smoked Shrimp*

Preparation Time: 10 minutes

Cooking Time: 20 minutes

Servings: 6

Ingredients:

- 1 lb. uncooked shrimp
- ½ tbsp. onion powder
- ½ tbsp. garlic powder
- 4 tbsp. mayo
- 2 tbsp. minced green onion
- ½ tbsp. salt

Directions:

1. Remove the shells from the shrimp and wash well.
2. Preheat the wood pellet grill to 450 degrees.
3. Season with garlic powder, onion powder, and salt.
4. Cook the shrimp for 5-6 minutes on each side.
5. Once cooked, remove the shrimp from the grill and garnish it with spring onion, teriyaki sauce, and mayo.

Nutrition: Amount per 51 g = 1 serving(s) Energy (calories): 62 kcal Protein: 8.21 g Fat: 2.17 g

Carbohydrates: 1.93 g

5. _Shrimp Wrapped in Bacon_

Preparation Time: 5 minutes

Cooking Time: 30 minutes

Servings: 12

Ingredients:

- 1 lb. raw shrimp

- ½ tbsp. garlic powder

- 1 lb. bacon (cut in half)

Directions:

1. Preheat your wood pellet grill to 350 degrees F.
2. Clean the shrimp by removing the shells and tails.
3. Wash and leave the shrimp to dry.
4. Sprinkle garlic powder and salt on the shrimp.
5. Wrap each shrimp with a slice of bacon and secure it using a toothpick.

6. Place a baking sheet on a tray. Place the shrimp wrapped in bacon on the tray.

7. Cook for 10 minutes, and then flip it to cook for another 10 minutes.

8. You can check if the bacon is crisp or leave it for another 5 minutes. Make sure you don't overcook it.

9. Remove it from the grill and serve with a nice dip.

Nutrition: Amount per 38 g = 1 serving(s) Energy (calories): 78 kcal Protein: 5.91 g Fat: 5.84 g Carbohydrates: 1.34 g

6. *Spicy Chicken Wings*

Preparation Time: 30 minutes

Cooking Time: 6 Hours

Servings: 1

Ingredients:

- For Hellfire chicken wings
- 3 lbs. of chicken wings
- 2 tablespoon of vegetable oil
- For the rub
- 1 teaspoon of onion powder
- 1 tablespoon of paprika
- 1 teaspoon of celery seed
- 1 teaspoon of salt
- 1 teaspoon of cayenne pepper
- 1 teaspoon of freshly ground black pepper
- 1 teaspoon of granulated garlic
- 2 teaspoons of brown sugar
- For the sauce
- 2 -4 thinly sliced crosswise jalapeno poppers

- 2 tablespoons of butter; unsalted
- ½ cup of hot sauce
- ½ cup of cilantro leaves

Directions:

1. Take the chicken wings and cut off the tips and discard them
2. Now cut each of the wings into two separate pieces through the joint
3. Move this in a large mixing bowl and pour oil right over it
4. For the rub: Take a small-sized bowl and add sugar, black pepper, paprika, onion powder, salt, celery seed, cayenne, and granulated garlic to it
5. Now sprinkle this mixture over the chicken and toss it gently to coat the wings thoroughly
6. Put the smoker to preheat by putting the temperature to 350 degrees F
7. Grill the wings for approximately 40 minutes or till the time the skin turns golden brown and you feel that it has cooked through. Make sure to turn it in once when you are halfway.
8. For the sauce: Take a small saucepan and melt the butter by keeping the flame on medium-low heat. Now add jalapenos to it and cook for 3 minutes, stir cilantro along with a hot sauce
9. Now, pour this freshly made sauce over the wings and toss it to coat well

10. Serve and enjoy

Nutrition: Carbohydrates: 27 g Protein: 19 g Sodium: 65 mg
Cholesterol: 49 mg

7. Buffalo Chicken Thighs

Preparation Time: 30 minutes

Cooking Time: 6 Hours

Servings: 1

Ingredients:

- 4-6 skinless, boneless chicken thighs
- Pork and poultry rub
- 4 tablespoons of butter
- 1 cup of sauce; buffalo wing
- Bleu cheese crumbles
- Ranch dressing

Directions:

1. Set the grill to preheat by keeping the temperature to 450 degrees F and keeping the lid closed
2. Now season the chicken thighs with the poultry rub and then place it on the grill grate
3. Cook it for 8 to 10 minutes while making sure to flip it once midway
4. Now take a small saucepan and cook the wing sauce along with butter by keeping the flame on medium heat. Make sure to stir in between to avoid lumps

5. Now take the cooked chicken and dip it into the wing sauce and the butter mix. Make sure to coat both sides in an even manner

6. Take the chicken thighs that have been sauced to the grill and then cook for further 15 minutes. Do so until the internal temperature reads 175 degrees

7. Sprinkle bleu cheese and drizzle the ranch dressing

8. Serve and enjoy

Nutrition: Carbohydrates: 29 Protein: 19 g Sodium: 25 mg Cholesterol: 19 mg

8. Sweet and Sour Chicken Drumsticks

Preparation Time: 30 minutes

Cooking Time: 2 Hours

Servings: 1

Ingredients:

- 8 pieces of chicken drumsticks
- 2 tablespoon of rice wine vinegar
- 3 tablespoon brown sugar
- 1 cup of ketchup
- ¼ cup of soy sauce
- Minced garlic
- 2 tablespoons of honey
- 1 tablespoon of sweet heat rub
- Minced ginger
- ½ lemon; juice
- 1/2 juiced lime

Directions:

1. Take a mixing bowl and add soy sauce along with brown sugar, ketchup, lemon, rice wine vinegar, sweet heat rub, honey, ginger, and garlic.
2. Now keep half of the mixture for dipping sauce and therefore set it aside

3. Take the leftover half and pour it in a plastic bag that can be re-sealed

4. Now add drumsticks to it and then seal the bag again

5. Refrigerate it for 4 to 12 hours

6. Take out the chicken from the bag and discard the marinade

7. Fire the grill and set the temperature to 225 degrees F

8. Now smoke the chicken over indirect heat for 2 to 3 hours a make sure to turn it in once or twice

9. Add more glaze if needed

10. Remove it from the grill and let it stand aside for 10 minutes

11. Add more sauce or keep it as a dipping sauce

12. Serve and enjoy

Nutrition: Carbohydrates: 29 g Protein: 19 g Sodium: 25 mg Cholesterol: 19 mg

9. *Smoked Whole Chicken with Honey Glaze*

Preparation Time: 30 minutes

Cooking Time: 3 Hours

Servings: 1

Ingredients:

- 1 4 pounds of chicken with the giblets thoroughly removed and patted dry
- 1 ½ lemon
- 1 tablespoon of honey
- 4 tablespoons of unsalted butter
- 4 tablespoon of chicken seasoning

Directions:

1. Fire up your smoker and set the temperature to 225 degrees F
2. Take a small saucepan and melt the butter along with honey over a low flame
3. Now squeeze ½ lemon in this mixture and then move it from the heat source
4. Take the chicken and smoke by keeping the skin side down. Do so until the chicken turns light brown and the skin starts to release from the grate.
5. Turn the chicken over and apply the honey butter mixture to it

6. Continue to smoke it making sure to taste it every 45 minutes until the thickest core reaches a temperature of 160 degrees F

7. Now remove the chicken from the grill and let it rest for 5 minutes

8. Serve with the leftover sliced lemon and enjoy

Nutrition: Carbohydrates: 29 g Protein: 19 g Sodium: 25 mg Cholesterol: 19 mg

10. *Slow Roasted Shawarma*

Preparation Time: 30 minutes

Cooking Time: 4 Hours

Servings: 1

Ingredients:

- 5 ½ lbs. of chicken thighs; boneless, skinless
- 4 ½ lbs. of lamb fat
- Pita bread
- 5 ½ lbs. of top sirloin
- 2 yellow onions; large
- 4 tablespoons of rub
- Desired toppings like pickles, tomatoes, fries, salad, and more

Directions:

1. Slice the meat and fat into ½" slices and place them in 3 separate bowls

2. Season each of the bowls with the rub and massage the rub into the meat to make sure it seeps well

3. Now place half of the onion at the base of each half skewer. This will make for a firm base

4. Add 2 layers from each of the bowls at a time

5. Make the track as symmetrical as you can

6. Now, put the other 2 half onions at the top of this

7. Wrap it in plastic wrap and let it refrigerate overnight

8. Set the grill to preheat keeping the temperature to 275 degrees F

9. Lay the shawarma on the grill grate and let it cook for approx. 4 hours. Make sure to turn it in at least once

10. Remove from the grill and shoot the temperature to 445 degrees F

11. Now place a cast iron pellet grill on the grill grate and pour it with olive oil

12. When the pellet grill has turned hot, place the whole shawarma on the cast iron and smoke it for 5 to 10 minutes per side

13. Remove from the grill and slice off the edges

14. Repeat the same with the leftover shawarma

15. Serve in pita bread and add the chosen toppings

16. Enjoy

Nutrition: Carbohydrates: 39 g Protein: 29 g Sodium: 15 mg Cholesterol: 19 mg

11. Duck Poppers

Preparation Time: 30 minutes

Cooking Time: 4 Hours

Servings: 1

Ingredients:

- 8 – 10 pieces of bacon, cut event into same-sized pieces measuring 4 inches each
- 3 duck breasts; boneless and with skin removed and sliced into strips measuring ½ inches
- Sriracha sauce
- 6 de-seeded jalapenos, with the top cut off and sliced into strips

Directions:

1. Wrap the bacon around one trip of pepper and one slice of duck
2. Secure it firmly with the help of a toothpick
3. Fire the grill on low flame and keep this wrap and grill it for half an hour until the bacon turns crisp
4. Rotate often to ensure even cooking
5. Serve with sriracha sauce

Nutrition: Carbohydrates: 39 g Protein: 29 g Sodium: 15 mg Cholesterol: 19 mg

12. BBQ Pulled Turkey Sandwiches

Preparation Time: 30 minutes

Cooking Time: 4 Hours

Servings: 1

Ingredients:

- 6 skin-on turkey thighs
- 6 split and buttered buns
- 1 ½ cups of chicken broth
- 1 cup of BBQ sauce
- Poultry rub

Directions:

1. Season the turkey thighs on both sides with poultry rub
2. Set the grill to preheat by pushing the temperature to 180 degrees F
3. Arrange the turkey thighs on the grate of the grill and smoke them for 30 minutes
4. Now transfer the thighs to an aluminum foil which is disposable and then pour the brine right around the thighs
5. Cover it with a lid
6. Now increase the grill, temperature to 325 degrees F and roast the thigh till the internal temperature reaches 180 degrees F
7. Remove the foil from the grill but do not turn off the grill
8. Let the turkey thighs cool down a little

9. Now pour the dripping and serve

10. Remove the skin and discard it

11. Pull the meat into shreds and return it to the foil

12. Add 1 more cup of BBQ sauce and some more dripping

13. Now cover the foil with a lid and re-heat the turkey on the smoker for half an hour

14. Serve and enjoy

Nutrition: Carbohydrates: 39 g Protein: 29 g Sodium: 15 mg Cholesterol: 19 mg

13. Baked Garlic Parmesan Wings

Preparation Time: 30 minutes

Cooking Time: 3 Hours

Servings: 1

Ingredients:

- For the chicken wings
- 5lbs. of chicken wings
- ½ cup of chicken rub
- For the garnish
- 1 cup of shredded parmesan cheese
- 3 tablespoons of chopped parsley
- For the sauce
- 10 cloves of finely diced garlic
- 1 cup of butter
- 2 tablespoon of chicken rub

Directions:

1. Set the grill on preheat by keeping the temperature to high
2. Take a large bowl and toss the wings in it along with the chicken rub
3. Now place the wings directly on the grill grate and cook it for 10 minutes
4. Flip it and cook for the ten minutes

5. Check the internal temperature and it needs to reach in the range of 165 to 180 degrees F
6. For the garlic sauce
7. Take a midsized saucepan and mix garlic, butter, and the leftover rub.
8. Cook it over medium heat on a stovetop
9. Cook for 10 minutes while stirring in between to avoid the making of lumps
10. Now when the wings have been cooked, remove them from the grill and place them in a large bowl
11. Toss the wings with garlic sauce along with parsley and parmesan cheese
12. Serve and enjoy

Nutrition: Carbohydrates: 19 g Protein: 29 g Sodium: 15 mg Cholesterol: 59 mg

BEEF RECIPES

14. Sweet & Spicy Beef Brisket

Preparation Time: 10 minutes

Cooking Time: 7 hours

Servings: 10

Ingredients:

- 1 cup paprika
- 3/4 cup sugar
- 3 tablespoons garlic salt
- 3 tablespoons onion powder
- 1 tablespoon celery salt
- 1 tablespoon lemon pepper
- 1 tablespoon ground black pepper
- 1 teaspoon cayenne pepper
- 1 teaspoon mustard powder
- ½ teaspoon dried thyme, crushed
- 1 (5-6-pound) beef brisket, trimmed

Directions:

1. In a bowl, place all ingredients except for beef brisket and mix well.
2. Rub the brisket with spice mixture generously.
3. With plastic wrap, cover the brisket and refrigerate overnight.

4. Preheat the Z Grills Wood Pellet Grill & Smoker on grill setting to 250 degrees F.

5. Place the brisket onto the grill over indirect heat and cook for about 3-3½ hours.

6. Flip and cook for about 3-3½ hours more.

7. Remove the brisket from the grill and place it onto a cutting board for about 10-15 minutes before slicing.

8. With a sharp knife, cut the brisket into desired-sized slices and serve.

Nutrition: Calories: 536 | Fat: 15g Cholesterol: 203mg | Carbs: 24g | Protein: 71g

15. *Beef Rump Roast*

Preparation Time: 10 minutes

Cooking Time: 6 hours

Servings: 8

Ingredients:

- 1 teaspoon smoked paprika
- 1 teaspoon cayenne pepper
- 1 teaspoon onion powder
- 1 teaspoon garlic powder
- Salt and ground black pepper, as required
- 3 pounds beef rump roast
- ¼ cup Worcestershire sauce

Directions:

1. Preheat the Z Grills Wood Pellet Grill & Smoker on the smoke setting to 200 degrees F, using charcoal.
2. In a bowl, mix all spices.
3. Coat the rump roast with Worcestershire sauce evenly and then, rub with spice mixture generously.
4. Place the rump roast onto the grill and cook for about 5-6 hours.
5. Remove the roast from the grill and place onto a cutting board for about 10-15 minutes before serving.

6. With a sharp knife, cut the roast into desired-sized slices and serve.

Nutrition: Calories: 252 | Fat: 9g Cholesterol: 113mg | Carbs: 2g | Protein: 37g

16. Spicy Chuck Roast

Preparation Time: 10 minutes

Cooking Time: 4 hours and 30 minutes

Servings: 8

Ingredients:

- 2 tablespoons onion powder
- 2 tablespoons garlic powder
- 1 tablespoon red chili powder
- 1 tablespoon cayenne pepper
- Salt and ground black pepper, as required
- 1 (3-pound) beef chuck roast
- 16 fluid ounces warm beef broth

Directions:

1. Preheat the grill setting to 250 degrees F.
2. In a bowl, mix spices, salt, and black pepper.
3. Rub the chuck roast with spice mixture evenly.
4. Place the rump roast onto the grill and cook for about 1½ hours per side.
5. Arrange chuck roast in a steaming pan with beef broth.
6. With a piece of foil, cover the pan and cook for about 2-3 hours.

7. Remove the chuck roast from the grill and place onto a cutting board for about 20 minutes before slicing.

8. With a sharp knife, cut the chuck roast into desired-sized slices and serve.

Nutrition: Calories: 645 | Fat: 48g Cholesterol: 175mg | Carbs: 4g | Protein: 46g

17. Smoked Rack Of Lamb

Preparation Time: 30 minutes

Cooking Time: 1 Hour and 15 Minutes

Servings: 4

Ingredients:

- 1rack of lamb rib, membrane removed
- For the Marinade:
- 1lemon, juiced
- 2teaspoons minced garlic
- 1teaspoon salt
- 1teaspoon ground black pepper
- 1teaspoon dried thyme
- ¼ cup balsamic vinegar
- 1teaspoon dried basil
- For the Glaze:
- 2tablespoons soy sauce
- ¼ cup Dijon mustard
- 2tablespoons Worcestershire sauce
- ¼ cup red wine

Directions:

1. Prepare the marinade and for this, take a small bowl, place all the ingredients in it and whisk until combined.

2. Place the rack of lamb into a large plastic bag, pour in marinade, seal it, turn it upside down to coat lamb with the marinade and let it marinate for a minimum of 8 hours in the refrigerator.

3. When ready to cook, switch on the grill, fill the grill hopper with flavored wood pellets, power the grill on by using the control panel, select 'smoke' on the temperature dial, or set the temperature to 300 degrees F and let it preheat for a minimum of 5 minutes.

4. Meanwhile, prepare the glaze and for this, take a small bowl, place all of its ingredients in it and whisk until combined.

5. When the grill has preheated, open the lid, place lamb rack on the grill grate, shut the grill, and smoke for 15 minutes.

6. Brush with glaze, flip the lamb and then continue smoking for 1 hour and 15 minutes until the internal temperature reaches 145 degrees F, basting with the glaze every 30 minutes.

7. When done, transfer lamb rack to a cutting board, let it rest for 15 minutes, cut it into slices, and then serve.

Nutrition: Calories: 323 Cal Fat: 18 g Carbs: 13 g Protein: 25 g Fiber: 1 g

18. Garlic Rack Of Lamb

Preparation Time: 30 minutes

Cooking Time: 3 Hours

Servings: 4

Ingredients:

- 1 rack of lamb, membrane removed
- For the Marinade:
- 2 teaspoons minced garlic
- 1 teaspoon dried basil
- 1/3 cup cream sherry
- 1 teaspoon dried oregano
- 1/3 cup Marsala wine
- 1 teaspoon dried rosemary
- ½ teaspoon ground black pepper
- 1/3 cup balsamic vinegar
- 2 tablespoons olive oil

Directions:

1. Prepare the marinade and for this, take a small bowl, place all of its ingredients in it and stir until well combined.
2. Place lamb rack in a large plastic bag, pour in marinade, seal the bag, turn it upside down to coat lamb with the marinade

and let it marinate for a minimum of 45 minutes in the refrigerator.

3. When ready to cook, switch on the grill, fill the grill hopper with flavored wood pellets, power the grill on by using the control panel, select 'smoke' on the temperature dial, or set the temperature to 250 degrees F and let it preheat for a minimum of 5 minutes.

4. Meanwhile,

5. When the grill has preheated, open the lid, place lamb rack on the grill grate, shut the grill, and smoke for 3 hours until the internal temperature reaches 165 degrees F.

6. When done, transfer lamb rack to a cutting board, let it rest for 10 minutes, then cut into slices and serve.

Nutrition: Calories: 210 Cal; Fat: 11 g; Carbs: 3 g; Protein: 25 g; Fiber: 1 g

19. Wine Braised Lamb Shank

Preparation Time: 30 minutes

Cooking Time: 10 Hours

Servings: 2

Ingredients:

- 2 (1¼-lb.) lamb shanks
- 1-2 C. water
- ¼ C. brown sugar
- 1/3 C. rice wine
- 1/3 C. soy sauce
- 1 tbsp. dark sesame oil
- 4 (1½x½-inch) orange zest strips
- 2 (3-inch long) cinnamon sticks
- 1½ tsp. Chinese five-spice powder

Directions:

1. Set the temperature of the Grill to 225-250 degrees F and preheat with a closed lid for 15 minutes., using charcoal and soaked applewood chips.
2. With a sharp knife, pierce each lamb shank at many places.
3. In a bowl, add remaining all ingredients and mix until sugar is dissolved.

4. In a large foil pan, place the lamb shanks and top with sugar mixture evenly.

5. Place the foil pan onto the grill and cook for about 8-10 hours, flipping after every 30 minutes. (If required, add enough water to keep the liquid ½-inch over).

6. Remove from the grill and serve hot.

Nutrition: Calories per serving: 1200; Carbohydrates: 39.7g; Protein: 161.9g; Fat: 48.4; Sugar: 29g; Sodium: 2000mg; Fiber: 0.3g

20. Crown Rack Of Lamb

Preparation Time: 15 minutes

Cooking Time: 30 Minutes

Servings: 6

Ingredients:

- 2 racks of lamb, frenched
- 1 tbsp. garlic, crushed
- 1 tbsp. rosemary, finely chopped
- 1/4 cup olive oil
- 2 feet twine

Directions:

1. Rinse the racks with cold water then pat them dry with a paper towel.
2. Lay the racks on a flat board then score between each bone, about 1/4 inch down.
3. In a mixing bowl, mix garlic, rosemary, and oil then generously brush on the lamb.
4. Take each lamb rack and bend it into a semicircle forming a crown-like shape.
5. Use the twine to wrap the racks about 4 times starting from the base to the top. Make sure you tie the twine tightly to keep the racks together.

6. Preheat the wood pellet to 400-450 F then place the lamb racks on a baking dish. Place the baking dish on the pellet grill.

7. Cook for 10 minutes then reduce temperature to 300 F. cook for 20 more minutes or until the internal temperature reaches 130 F.

8. Remove the lamb rack from the wood pellet and let rest for 15 minutes.

9. Serve when hot with veggies and potatoes. Enjoy.

Nutrition: Calories 390, Total fat 35g, Saturated fat 15g, Total Carbs 0g, Net Carbs 0g, Protein 17g, Sugar 0g, Fiber 0g, Sodium: 65mg.

21. Hickory-Smoked Prime Rib of Pork

Preparation Time: 30 minutes

Cooking Time: 3 hours

Servings: 6

Ingredients:

- Pellet: Hickory
- 1 (5-pound) rack of pork, around 6 ribs
- ¼ cup roasted garlic–enhanced extra-virgin olive oil
- 6 tablespoons Jan's Original Dry Rub, Pork Dry Rub, or your preferred pork roast rub

Directions:

1. Trim of the fat cap and silver skin from the rack of pork. Much the same as a chunk of ribs a rack of pork has a membrane on the bones. Remove the membrane from the bones by working a spoon handle under the bone membrane until you can get the membrane with a paper towel to pull it off.

2. Rub the olive oil generously on all sides of the meat. Season with the rub, covering all sides of the meat.

3. Double wrap the seasoned rack of pork in plastic wrap and refrigerate for 2 to 4 hours or medium-term.

4. Remove the seasoned rack of pork from the refrigerator and let sit at room temperature for 30 minutes before cooking.

5. Arrange the wood pellet smoker-grill for non-direct cooking and preheat to 225°F utilizing hickory pellets.

6. Add your wood pellet smoker-grill meat probe or a remote meat probe into the thickest part of the rack of pork. On the off chance that your grill doesn't have meat probe capabilities or you don't claim a remote meat probe at that point, utilize a moment-read computerized thermometer during the cook for internal temperature readings.

7. Place the rack rib-side down directly on the grill grates.

8. Smoke the rack of pork for 3 to 3½ hours, until the internal temperature arrives at 140°F.

9. Remove the meat from the smoker, and let it rest under a free foil tent for 15 minutes before cutting.

Nutrition: Calories: 189 kCal   Protein: 17 g   Fat: 12 g

22. *Tender Grilled Loin Chops*

Preparation Time: 10 minutes

Cooking Time: 12 to 15 minutes

Servings: 6

Ingredients:

- Pellet: Any
- 6 boneless focus cut midsection pork cleaves, 1 to 1½ inches thick 2 quarts Pork Brine
- 2 tablespoons roasted garlic–seasoned extra-virgin olive oil
- 2 teaspoons black pepper

Directions:

1. Trim abundance fat and silver skin from the pork slashes.
2. Place the pork slashes and brine in a 1-gallon sealable pack and refrigerate for in any event 12 hours or medium-term.
3. Remove the pork slashes from the brine and pat them dry with paper towels.
4. Brined pork hacks cook quicker than un-brined cleaves, so be mindful to screen internal temperatures.
5. Rest the pork slashes under a foil tent for 5 minutes before serving.

Nutrition: Calories: 211 kCal   Protein: 17 g   Fat: 21 g

23. *Florentine Ribeye Pork Loin*

Preparation Time: 30 minutes

Cooking Time: 60 to 75 minutes

Servings: 6 to 8

Ingredients:

- 1 (3-pound) boneless ribeye pork loin roast
- 4 tablespoons extra-virgin olive oil, divided
- 2 tablespoons Pork Dry Rub or your favorite pork seasoning
- 4 bacon slices
- 6 cups fresh spinach
- 1 small red onion, diced
- 6 cloves garlic, cut into thin slivers
- ¾ cup shredded mozzarella cheese

Directions:

1. Trim away any abundance of fat and silver skin.
2. Butterfly the pork loin or approach your butcher to butterfly it for you. There are numerous phenomenal recordings online with nitty-gritty directions on the various systems for butterflying a loin roast.
3. Rub 2 tablespoons of olive oil on each side of the butterflied roast and season the two sides with the rub.

4. Cook the bacon in a large skillet over medium heat. Disintegrate and set aside. Reserve the bacon fat.

5. Grill the pork loin for 60 to 75 minutes, or until the internal temperature at the thickest part arrives at 140°F.

6. Rest the pork loin under a free foil tent for 15 minutes before cutting contrary to what would be expected.

Nutrition: Calories: 365 kCal Protein: 32.1 g Fat: 22 g

24. Naked St. Louis Ribs

Preparation Time: 30 minutes

Cooking Time: 5 to 6 hours

Servings: 6 to 8

Ingredients:

- Pellet: Hickory, Apple
- 3 St. Louis–style pork rib racks
- 1 cup in addition to 1 tablespoon Jan's Original Dry Rub or your preferred pork rub

Directions:

1. Remove the membrane on the underside of the rib racks by embedding a spoon handle between the membrane and rib bones. Get the membrane with a paper towel and gradually dismantle it down the rack to remove.
2. Rub the two sides of the ribs with a liberal measure of the rub.
3. Arrange the wood pellet smoker-grill for non-direct cooking and preheat to 225°F utilizing hickory or apple pellets.
4. In the event of utilizing a rib rack, place the ribs in the rack on the grill grates. Else you can utilize Teflon-covered fiberglass tangles or place the ribs directly on the grill grates.
5. Smoke the ribs at 225°F for 5 to 6 hours with hickory pellets until the internal temperature, at the thickest part of the ribs, arrives at 185°F to190°F.

6. Rest the ribs under a free foil tent for 10 minutes before cutting and serving.

Nutrition: Calories: 241kCal   Protein: 23.6 g   Fat: 13 g

25. Buttermilk Pork Sirloin Roast

Preparation Time: 20 minutes

Cooking Time: 3 to 3½ hours

Servings: 4 to 6

Ingredients:

- Pellet: Apple, Cherry
- 1 (3 to 3½-pound) pork sirloin roast

Directions:

1. Trim all fat and silver skin from the pork roast.
2. Place the roast and buttermilk brine in a 1-gallon sealable plastic sack or bringing holder.
3. Refrigerate medium-term, turning the roast like clockwork whenever the situation allows.
4. Remove the brined pork sirloin roast from the brine and pat dry with a paper towel.
5. Supplement a meat probe into the thickest part of the roast.
6. Design the wood pellet smoker-grill for non-direct cooking and preheat to 225°F utilizing apple or cherry pellets.
7. Smoke the roast until the internal temperature arrives at 145°F, 3 to 3½ hours.
8. Rest the roast under a free foil tent for 15 minutes, at that point cut contrary to what would be expected.

Nutrition: Calories: 311 kCal   Protein: 25 g   Fat: 18 g

26. *Baby Bok Choy with Lime-Miso Vinaigrette*

Preparation Time: 10 minutes

Cooking Time: 25 minutes

Servings: 4

Ingredients:

- ¼ cup good-quality vegetable oil
- Grated zest of 1 lime
- 2 tablespoons fresh lime juice
- 2 tablespoons white or light miso
- 1 tablespoon rice vinegar
- Salt and pepper
- 1½ pounds baby bok choy

Directions:

1. Start the coals or heat a gas grill for medium direct cooking. Make sure the grates are clean.

2. Whisk the oil, lime zest and juice, miso, and vinegar together in a small bowl until combined and thickened. Taste and adjust the seasoning with salt and pepper.

3. Trim the bottoms from the bok choy and cut them into halves or quarters as needed. Pour half the vinaigrette into a large baking dish. Add the bok choy and turn in the vinaigrette until completely coated.

4. Put the bok choy on the grill directly over the fire. Close the lid and cook, turning once, until the leaves brown, and you can insert a knife through the core with no resistance, 5 to 10 minutes per side, depending on their size. Transfer to a platter; drizzle with the reserved vinaigrette and serve warm or at room temperature.

Nutrition: Calories: 209.7 Fats: 9.4 g Cholesterol: 7.4 mg Carbohydrates: 25.9 g Fiber: 4.5 g Sugars: 3 g Proteins: 10.1 g

27. Grilled Carrots

Preparation Time: 5 minutes,

Cooking Time: 20 minutes

Servings: 6

Ingredients:

- 1 lb. carrots, large
- 1/2 tbsp. salt
- 6 oz. butter
- 1/2 tbsp. black pepper
- Fresh thyme

Directions:

1. Thoroughly wash the carrots and do not peel. Pat them dry and coat with olive oil.
2. Add salt to your carrots.
3. Meanwhile, preheat a pellet grill to 350oF.
4. Now place your carrots directly on the grill or on a raised rack.
5. Close and cook for about 20 minutes.
6. While carrots cook, cook butter in a saucepan, small, over medium heat until browned. Stir constantly to avoid it from burning. Remove from heat.
7. Remove carrots from the grill onto a plate then drizzle with browned butter.

8. Add pepper and splash with thyme.

9. Serve and enjoy.

Nutrition: Calories: 250 Total Fat: 25 g Saturated Fat: 15 g Total Carbs: 6 g Net Carbs: 4g Protein: 1 g Sugars: 3 g Fiber: 2 g Sodium: 402 mg

28. Wood pellet Spicy Brisket

Preparation Time: 20 minutes

Cooking Time: 9 hours

Servings: 10

Ingredients:

- 2 tbsp. garlic powder
- 2 tbsp. onion powder
- 2 tbsp. paprika
- 2 tbsp. chili powder
- 1/3 cup salt
- 1/3 cup black pepper
- 12 lb. whole packer brisket, trimmed
- 1-1/2 cup beef broth

Directions:

1. Set your wood pellet temperature to 225°F. Let preheat for 15 minutes with the lid closed.
2. Meanwhile, mix garlic, onion, paprika, chili, salt, and pepper in a mixing bowl.
3. the brisket generously on all sides.
4. Place the meat on the grill with the fat side down and let it cool until the internal temperature reaches 160°F.

5. Remove the meat from the grill and double wrap it with foil. Return it to the grill and cook until the internal temperature reaches 204°F.

6. Remove from grill, unwrap the brisket and let rest for 15 minutes.

7. Slice and serve.

Nutrition: Calories: 270 Total Fat: 20 g Saturated Fat: 8 g Total Carbs: 3 g Net Carbs: 3 g Protein: 20 g Sugar: 1 g Fiber: 0 g Sodium: 1220mg

29. Pellet Grill Funeral Potatoes

Preparation Time: 10 minutes

Cooking Time: 1 hour

Servings: 8

Ingredients:

- 1, 32 oz., package frozen hash browns
- 1/2 cup cheddar cheese, grated
- 1 can cream of chicken soup
- 1 cup sour cream
- 1 cup Mayonnaise
- 3 cups corn flakes, whole or crushed
- 1/4 cup melted butter

Directions:

1. Preheat your pellet grill to 350oF.
2. Spray a 13 x 9 baking pan, aluminum, using a cooking spray, non-stick.
3. Mix hash browns, cheddar cheese, chicken soup cream, sour cream, and mayonnaise in a bowl, large.
4. Spoon the mixture into a baking pan gently.
5. Mix corn flakes and melted butter then sprinkle over the casserole.

6. Grill for about 1-1/2 hours until potatoes become tender. If the top browns too much, cover using a foil until potatoes are done.

7. Remove from the grill and serve hot.

Nutrition: Calories: 403 Total Fat: 37 g Saturated Fat: 12 g Total Carbs: 14 g Net Carbs: 14 g Protein: 4 g Sugars: 2 g Fiber: 0 g Sodium: 620 mg

30. Smoked Cashews

Preparation Time: 5 minutes

Cooking Time: 1 hour

Servings 4 to 6

Ingredients:

- 1 pound (454 g) roasted, salted cashews

Directions:

1. Supply your smoker with wood pellets and follow the manufacturer's specific start-up procedure. Preheat the grill, with the lid closed, to 120°F (49°C).

2. Pour the cashews onto a rimmed baking sheet and smoke for 1 hour, stirring once about halfway through the smoking time.

3. Remove the cashews from the grill, let cool, and store them in an airtight container for as long as you can resist.

Nutrition: Calories: 57 Total Fat: 3 g Saturated Fat: 1 g Total Carbs: 6 g Net Carbs: 4 g Protein: 4 g Sugars: 2 g Fiber: 2 g Sodium: 484 mg

31. Smoked Volcanic Potatoes

Preparation Time: 15 minutes

Cooking Time: 3 hours

Servings: 4

Ingredients:

- 2 russet potatoes
- ¾ cup sour cream
- 1 cup cheddar cheese
- 2 tablespoons green onion
- 8 bacon strips
- 4 tablespoons butter
- 2 tablespoons olive oil
- Salt as needed

Directions:

1. Take your drip pan and add water; cover with aluminum foil. Preheat your smoker to 200 degrees F. Use water to fill the water pan halfway through and place it over the drip pan. Add wood chips to the side tray.

2. Take oil and salt, rub on potatoes and wrap potatoes in foil. Transfer to the smoker. Smoke for 3 hours, cut off each potato's top, and remove potato flesh and leave shell empty.

3. Fry and crumble the bacon; add potato flesh with bacon, butter, sour cream, cheese in a bowl. Add prepared filling into the potatoes, add cheese on top.

4. Wrap potato with 2 bacon slices, secure with a toothpick. Smoke for 1 hour more. Add green onions with little sour cream on top. Serve and enjoy!

Nutrition: Calories: 222 Carbs: 48g Fat: 2g Protein: 6g

32. Smoky-Sweet Potatoes

Preparation Time: 15 minutes

Cooking Time: 2-3 hours

Servings: 6

Ingredients:

- 6 sweet potatoes, scrubbed, eyes removed
- Extra-virgin olive oil
- Sea salt
- Butter
- Black pepper

Directions:

1. Preheat your electric smoker to 250°F. First, using a metal fork, pierce the unpeeled sweet potatoes several times. Brush them using olive oil, then season with sea salt.
2. Position the potatoes on the top rack and smoke for between 2-3 hours, until fork-tender and oozing. Serve the potatoes slathered with butter and seasoned with salt and pepper.

Nutrition: Calories: 282 Carbs: 51g Fat: 7g Protein: 5g

33. *Smoked Squash Casserole*

Preparation Time: 15 minutes

Cooking Time: 40 minutes

Servings: 2

Ingredients:

- 2½ lbs. yellow squash
- 2 tbsps. parsley flakes
- 2 eggs, beaten
- 1 medium yellow onion
- 1 sleeve saltine crackers
- 1 package Velveeta cheese
- ½ cup Alouette Sundried Tomato
- Basil cheese spread
- ¼ cup Alouette Garlic and Herb cheese spread
- ¼ cup mayonnaise
- ¾ tsp. hot sauce
- ¼ tsp. Cajun seasoning
- ½ cup butter
- ¼ tsp. salt
- ¼ tsp. black pepper

Directions:

1. Preheat the electric smoker to 250 F. Combine squash and onion in a large saucepan and add water to cover. Boil on medium heat until tender.

2. Drain and to this hot mixture, add Velveeta cheese, Alouette cheese, mayonnaise, parsley flakes, hot sauce, Cajun seasoning, salt, and pepper to taste. Stir all together well.

3. Cool a little, add eggs and stir until mixed. Melt butter in a saucepan. Add crushed crackers to the butter and stir well. Combine ½ cup of butter-cracker mix with the squash mixture. Stir thoroughly.

4. Pour into a disposable aluminum foil pan, then top the squash with the remaining butter and crackers. Cover the pan tightly with aluminum foil.

5. Put on the lower rack of the smoker and cook for 1 hr. Put one small handful of prepared wood chips in the wood tray for the best result, use hickory.

6. After an hour, remove the foil from the casserole and cook for another 15 minutes.

Nutrition: Calories: 65 Carbs: 8g Fat: 1g Protein: 5g

34. Smoked Salsa

Preparation Time: 15 minutes

Cooking Time: 30 minutes

Servings: 2

Ingredients:

- 3 tomatoes, diced
- 4 jalapenos, diced
- ½ onion, diced
- 4 cloves of garlic, minced
- 1 tablespoon cilantro
- 1 lime, juiced
- Salt to taste

Directions:

1. Preheat, the smoker to 225F. Put water in the water pan and add applewood chips into the side tray.
2. Combine all fixings and place them in an aluminum pan. Smoke for 30 minutes. Chill before serving with tortilla chips.

Nutrition: Calories: 212 Carbs: 28g Fat: 9g Protein: 3g

35. Smoked Baked Beans

Preparation Time: 15 minutes

Cooking Time: 2-3 hours

Servings: 6-8

Ingredients:

- 6 slices bacon, cut widthwise into 1/4" pieces
- 1 large yellow/white onion, finely chopped
- 1 red/green bell pepper, chopped into small bite-size
- 2 cloves garlic, minced
- 3 15-ounce cans of Great Northern beans, drained & rinsed
- 1/3 cup packed dark brown sugar
- 1/3 cup ketchup
- 1/4 cup dark molasses
- 2-1/2 tbsp apple cider vinegar, preferably unfiltered
- 2 tbsp Worcestershire sauce
- 1-1/2 tbsp Dijon mustard
- Salt
- ground black pepper
- 3/4 cup dark beer/water (not added all at once)

Directions:

1. In a heavy oven-proof pot, sauté the bacon over medium heat within 5 minutes. Drain off all except for 2 tablespoons of the bacon fat.

2. Put the onion, bell pepper, plus garlic, and cook within 5 minutes. Mix in the beans, sugar, ketchup, molasses, vinegar, Worcestershire sauce, plus mustard.

3. Put salt plus pepper to taste. Mix in some of the beer or water, then reserve the rest for adding later, if needed.

4. Warm your smoker to 225°F with the top vent open, then put water to half full in the bottom bowl. Put wood chips on the side tray.

5. Put the pot on a rack inside your smoker, uncovered. Smoke within 2 to 3 hours.

6. Mix occasionally and put more beer or water as needed if the beans are drying out too much. Remember to replenish the wood chips and water as needed, approximately every 60 minutes.

Nutrition: Calories: 150 Carbs: 29g Fat: 1g Protein: 7g

36. Beef Burgers

Preparation Time: 5 Minutes

Cooking Time: 4 Minutes

Servings: 4

Ingredients:

- 1¼ pounds lean ground beef
- 1 small onion, minced
- ¼ cup teriyaki sauce
- 3 tablespoons I thalian-flavored bread crumbs
- 2 tablespoons grated Parmesan cheese
- 1 teaspoon salt
- 1 teaspoon freshly ground black pepper
- 3 tablespoons sweet pickle relish
- 4 Kaiser rolls, toasted

Directions:

1. Put the beef in a medium bowl and add the onion, teriyaki sauce, bread crumbs, Parmesan cheese, salt, and pepper. Using a fork, mix the seasonings into the meat and then form the mixture into 4 patties, each about 1 inch thick.

2. Bring the pellet grill to high heat. When the pellet grill is hot place the burgers and cook for 4 minutes without flipping. Remove the burgers and cover to keep warm. Top each

burger with a spoonful of sweet pickle relish before sandwiching between a bun. Serve immediately.

Nutrition: Calories: 519; Fat: 23g; Protein: 33g

37. Tzatziki Lamb Burgers

Preparation Time: 5 Minutes

Cooking Time:12 Minutes

Servings: 5

Ingredients:

- 1½ pounds boneless lamb shoulder or leg or good-quality ground lamb
- 1 tablespoon chopped fresh oregano
- 1 teaspoon salt
- 1 teaspoon black pepper
- 1 tablespoon minced garlic
- ½ cup Greek yogurt
- 1 tablespoon olive oil, plus more for brushing
- 1 tablespoon red wine vinegar
- 2 tablespoons crumbled feta cheese
- 4 or 5 ciabatta rolls, split, or 8–10 slider buns (like potato or dinner rolls)
- Thinly sliced cucumbers for serving

Directions:

1. Put the lamb, oregano, salt, pepper, and garlic in a food processor and pulse until coarsely ground—finer than chopped, but not much. (If you're using pre-ground meat, put

it in a bowl with the seasonings and work them together gently with your hands.) Take a bit of the mixture and fry it up to taste for seasoning; adjust if necessary. Handling the meat as little as possible to avoid compressing it, shape the mixture lightly into 4 or 5 burgers or 8 to 10 sliders. Refrigerate the burgers until you're ready to pellet grill; if you make them several hours in advance, cover with plastic wrap.

2. Whisk the yogurt, oil, and vinegar together in a small bowl until smooth. Stir in the feta. Taste and adjust the seasoning with salt and pepper.

3. Bring the pellet grill to high heat. When the pellet grill is hot, place the burgers and cook for 11 minutes.

4. Transfer the burgers to a plate. Brush the cut sides of the rolls lightly with oil and toast directly over the pellet grill, 1 to 2 minutes. Top with a burger, then several slices of cucumber, a dollop of the sauce, and the other half of the roll. Serve with the remaining sauce on the side.

Nutrition: Calories: 134; Fat: 21g; Protein:36g; Fiber:2g

38. New Mexican Salsa Verde

Preparation Time: 5 Minutes

Cooking Time: 15 Minutes

Servings: 1 Cup

Ingredients:

- cloves garlic (leave the skins on),
- skewered on a wooden toothpick or small bamboo skewer
- 1 cup roasted New Mexican green chiles or Anaheim chiles cut into ¼-inch strips (8 to 10 chiles
- 2 tablespoons chopped fresh cilantro
- 2 teaspoons fresh lime juice, or more to taste
- ½ teaspoon ground cumin
- ½ teaspoon dried oregano
- Coarse salt (kosher or sea) and freshly
- ground black pepper

Directions:

1. Preheat the pellet grill to high. When ready to cook, lightly oil the pellet grill surface. Place the burgers on the hot pellet grill. The burgers will be done after cooking for 4 to 6 minutes. Put the garlic cloves until they are lightly browned and tender, 2 to 3 minutes per side (4 to 6 minutes in all). Scrape any burnt skin off the garlic. Place the garlic, chile strips, cilantro, lime

juice, cumin, oregano, and 4 tablespoons of water in a blender and purée until smooth, scraping down the sides of the blender with a spatula.

2. Transfer the salsa to a saucepan and bring to a gentle simmer over medium heat. Let simmer until thick and flavorful, 5 to 8 minutes, stirring with a wooden spoon. The salsa should be thick (roughly the consistency of heavy cream) but pourable; add more water as needed. Taste for seasoning, adding more lime juice as necessary and salt and pepper to taste; the salsa should be highly seasoned.

Nutrition: Calories: 214; Fat: 16g; Protein:36g; Fiber:2g

39. Chipotle Burgers With Avocado

Preparation Time: 5 Minutes

Cooking Time: 5 Minutes

Servings: 4

Ingredients:

- 1¼ pounds lean ground beef
- 2 tablespoons chipotle puree
- ½ teaspoon salt
- ¼ teaspoon freshly ground black pepper
- slices cheddar cheese (about 4 ounces)
- 1 avocado, halved, pitted, and sliced
- ¼ head iceberg lettuce, shredded
- 4 hamburger buns, toasted

Directions:

1. Put the beef in a medium bowl and add the chipotle puree, salt, and pepper. Using a fork, mix the seasonings into the meat and then, with your hands, form the mixture into 4 patties, each about 1 inch thick.

2. Turn the control knob to the high position, when the pellet grill is hot, place the burgers and cook for 4 minutes without flipping. Topping each burger with a slice of cheese and cook

for 1 minute more, until the cheese melts. Remove the burgers and cover to keep warm.

3. Top each burger with a few slices of avocado and some shredded lettuce before sandwiching between a bun.

4. Chipotle Puree: Put canned chipotles and their liquid in a blender or food processor and process until smooth. The puree can be covered with plastic wrap and refrigerated for up to 2 weeks. This stuff is hot-hot-hot, so a little goes a long way. I use it in meat marinades and dips. The puree is sold in some grocery stores, in the ethnic mark.

Nutrition: Calories: 590; Fat: 38g; Protein: 37g

40. Low Carb Almond Flour Bread

Preparation Time: 10 minutes

Cooking Time: 1 hour 15 minutes

Servings: 24 slices

Ingredients:

- 1 tsp sea salt or to taste
- 1 tbsp apple cider vinegar
- ½ cup of warm water
- ¼ cup of coconut oil
- 4 large eggs (beaten)
- 1 tbsp gluten-free baking powder
- 2 cup blanched almond flour
- ¼ cup Psyllium husk powder
- 1 tsp ginger (optional)

Directions:

1. Preheat the grill to 350°F with the lid closed for 15 minutes.
2. Line a 9 by 5-inch loaf pan with parchment paper. Set aside.
3. Combine the ginger, Psyllium husk powder, almond flour, salt, baking powder in a large mixing bowl.
4. In another mixing bowl, mix the coconut oil, apple cider vinegar, eggs, and warm water. Mix thoroughly.

5. Gradually pour the flour mixture into the egg mixture, stirring as you pour. Stir until it forms a smooth batter.

6. Fill the lined loaf pan with the batter and cover the batter with aluminum foil.

7. Place the loaf pan directly on the grill and bake for about 1 hour or until a toothpick or knife inserted in the middle of the bread comes out clean.

Nutrition: Calories: 93 | Total Fat: 7.5g | Saturated Fat: 2.6g Cholesterol: 31mg | Sodium: 139mg

Total Carbohydrate: 3.6g Dietary Fiber: 2.2g Total Sugars: 0.1g | Protein: 3.1g

CPSIA information can be obtained
at www.ICGtesting.com
Printed in the USA
BVHW041026240721
612638BV00010B/1053

9 781803 050102